Name Your

HERO

Lynn Lemley

DEDICATION

To my Dad who couldn't be here and my
Mom who never stopped believing.

ACKNOWLEDGMENTS

Special thanks to Ancestry.com which allowed me access hundreds of years of names.

Table of Contents

Introduction

Crafting a character is one of the key elements in writing a novel. Most authors usually have a personality in mind for a character long before they begin piecing the story together. Once that personality is in place a writer faces the daunting task of naming their character. Sometimes a run-of-the-mill name will do the trick, but more often than not you need a name that will encompass not only the character's identifying traits but the time period they live in.

It's time to write that story. Now, what do you name your hero?

Do you find yourself spending hours contemplating just the right name for your character? Do you dread sifting through thousands of names in run-of-the-mill baby name books? At some point, most writers wrack their brains or lose themselves in name research all in a quest for the perfect name for their hero; one that will encompass and amplify the persona of their larger-than-life character.

Deciding on the ideal name for your leading man gives the reader as much of a "sense" of the man as the physical and personality description revealed in the story. Strong names feed the reader's confidence in a story's hero and focus the reader's attention on the hero's actions.

Name Your Hero is *the* reference book for writers searching for that perfect hyper-masculine name for the leading male character(s) in their great American Novel – or even a short story.

Don't waste time with ordinary name books; reach for *Name Your Hero* - the one tool designed to help you name your leading man.

"A"

Aakarshan
Aaron
Abaddon
Abba
Abban
Abbas
Abbott
Abdel
Abdiel
Abdieso
Abdul
Abdullah
Abe
Abejundio
Abel
Abelard
Abell
Abenzio
Abercio
Abernethy
Abhay
Abhi
Abhijit
Abhinav
Abhishek
Abhorson
Abi
Abie
Abiel

Abijah
Abir
Abisha
Abner
Abraham
Abram
Abrasha
Absalom
Abudemio
Abundiantus
Acacio
Acario
Accursius
Ace
Acelin
Achilles
Achyuta
Ackerley
Ackley
Ackworth
Acton
Acuzio
Adair
Adalardo
Adalgiso
Adalrico
Adam
Adams
Adar
Addai
Addicock
Addison

Addo
Adeben
Adeipho
Adel
Adelais
Adelard
Adelbert
Adelfried
Adelino
Adelmo
Adelphos
Ademaro
Aden
Adeodatus
Adhamh
Adin
Adir
Adiran
Aditya
Adlai
Adler
Adley
Admes
Admon
Adnan
Adney
Adolfo
Adolph
Adon
Adoni
Adonis
Adony

Adrastos	Ajatashatru	Albin
Adrian	Ajax	Albion
Adriel	Ajayi	Alcander
Aegeon	Ajit	Alcibiades
Aemilius	Ajitabh	Alcott
Aeneas	Akaash	Aldebourne
Aeolus	Akama	Alden
Aeron	Akando	Alder
Aetos	Akbar	Alderney
Afro	Akello	Aldous
Agabo	Akil	Aldred
Agamemnon	Akim	Aldrich
Agatone	Akira	Aldridge
Agilard	Akiva	Aldwin
Agosto	Akiyama	Aldwyn
Agrippa	Akram	Alec
Agu	Aksel	Aled
Agustin	Akshay	Alejandro
Ahab	Al	Aleron
Ahearn	Aladdin	Aleser
Ahmed	Alan	Alessandro
Ahmik	Aland	Alex
Ahren	Alarbus	Alexander
Aidan	Alard	Alexas
Aiken	Alaric	Alexis
Ailen	Alasdair	Alfons
Aimery	Alastair	Alfonso
Aimon	Alban	Alford
Aindreas	Alber	Alfray
Ainsley	Alberich	Alfred
Aitan	Albern	Alger
Ajani	Albert	Algernon

Algren	Alwan	Amol
Ali	Alwin	Amon
Alicock	Alwyn	Amondsham
Alika	Amadeus	Amory
Alim	Amadi	Amos
Alison	Amado	Amrit
Alistair	Amador	Amsden
Alister	Amal	Amul
Allambee	Amar	Amulya
Allan	Amaro	Amund
Allard	Amaroo	Anand
Allen	Amato	Anant
Alleyne	Ambar	Anastasius
Allighiero	Amberden	Anatole
Allington	Ambert	Anay
Allister	Ambler	Ancel
Almo	Ambrose	Anders
Almon	Amcotts	Anderson
Alok	Amery	Andreus
Alonso	Amherst	Andrew
Aloysius	Amida	Andrews
Alphonse	Amiel	Androcles
Alphonso	Amiens	Aneurin
Alric	Amin	Ang
Alroy	Amir	Angada
Alston	Amiri	Angelo
Altair	Amirov	Angus
Altman	Amistad	Angwyn
Alun	Amit	Anieli
Alvah	Amitabh	Anil
Alvin	Amitava	Anirudhh
Alvis	Ammon	Anish

Aniston	Anwell	Aric
Anjuman	Anyon	Aricin
Anker	Apache	Ariel
Ankit	Apari	Ariki
Ankur	Apemantus	Arion
Annan	Apollo	Aristedes
Annesley	Apostolos	Aristo
Anniruddha	Aquila	Aristotle
Anno	Ara	Arizona
Anoke	Araluen	Arje
Anoki	Aram	Arjun
Anoop	Aran	Arkin
Ansari	Arana	Arkwright
Anscom	Archard	Arland
Ansel	Archer	Arlen
Anselm	Archibald	Arley
Anshul	Archibold	Arlo
Anshuman	Archidamus	Armand
Ansley	Archie	Armande
Anson	Ardall	Armando
Anstice	Arden	Armen
Ansty	Ardern	Armon
Antal	Ardley	Armstrong
Anthony	Ardolph	Arnall
Antigonus	Ardon	Arnaud
Antiochus	Aren	Arne
Antipholus	Arend	Arnett
Anton	Ares	Arnie
Antoni	Argentein	Arnold
Antonio	Argus	Arnon
Anu	Argyll	Aron
Anwar	Ari	Aronne

Aroon	Ashliegh	Atherol
Arpiar	Ashlin	Atherton
Arran	Ashok	Athol
Arsen	Ashon	Athos
Arsenio	Ashraf	Atilla
Art	Ashton	Atiu
Arthur	Ashur	Atkinson
Arthus	Ashutosh	Atlas
Artie	Ashwin	Atlee
Arty	Ashwini	Atley
Aruiragus	Asija	Atmajyoti
Arun	Asim	Atman
Arundel	Askel	Atrayl
Arunta	Askew	Atrus
Arvad	Aslak	Attila
Arval	Asparouh	Attilburgh
Arvin	Asplin	Attis
Arvind	Astin	Atul
Arviragus	Astley	Atulya
Arwin	Aston	Atwater
Asa	Asuman	Atwell
Ascot	Asvathama	Atworth
Aseem	Asvin	Auberon
Asger	Aswad	Aubert
Ash	Aswin	Aubin
Ashburn	Asztrik	Aubrey
Ashby	Atalik	Auburn
Ashcombe	Atarah	Audeley
Ashenhurst	Atawn	Audlington
Asher	Athan	Audric
Ashford	Atharvan	Audun
Ashish	Athelstan	August

Augustine

Augustus

Aurek

Aurelio

Aurelius

Austell

Austen

Austin

Autolucus

Avan

Avel

Avenall

Averell

Averill

Avery

Avinash

Aviv

Avner

Avon

Avram

Avrom

Axel

Axton

Ayde

Ayer

Ayhner

Ayleward

Aylmer

Aylward

Aylwin

Aynesworth

Ayush

Azariah

Azi

Azim

Aziz

Azriel

Azzan

"B"

Babar

Babham

Babington

Babul

Bacchus

Badby

Bae

Bahar

Bailey

Baingana

Baird

Bairn

Bajnok

Bakari

Baker

Balam

Balavan

Balbo

Balder

Baldric

Baldwin

Bale

Balfour

Bali

Balint

Ballard

Ballett

Balram

Balthasar

Balthazar

Balun

Bammard

Bancroft

Bandele

Bane

Banjora

Bankim

Banning

Banquo

Bansi

Baptista

Barabas

Barak

Baran

Barber

Barclay

Barden

Bardo

Bardolf

Bardolph

Bardon

Barefoot

Barega

Barend

Bari
Barker
Barlow
Barna
Barnabas
Barnaby
Barnard
Barnardine
Barnardo
Barnes
Barnet
Barnett
Barney
Barnum
Barny
Baron
Barre
Barrentine
Barrett
Barry
Bars
Barse
Barstaple
Bart
Bartelot
Barth
Bartholomew
Bartho
Barton
Baruch
Barwon
Bashir

Basil
Basim
Bassanio
Basset
Bassett
Bastiaan
Bastian
Bastien
Bates
Bathurst
Battersby
Battle
Baudouin
Baul
Bavol
Baxter
Bay
Bayanai
Bayard
Bayley
Baynton
Bazyli
Beacan
Beacher
Beagan
Beaman
Beardsley
Beathan
Beattie
Beau
Beauchamp
Beaumont

Beauregard
Beaurepaire
Bebe
Becan
Beck
Beckingham
Becse
Bede
Bedell
Bedgberry
Bedingfeld
Bedrich
Beeton
Bela
Belarius
Beldon
Belen
Bell
Bellamy
Bem
Bemus
Ben
Bence
Bend
Benedick
Benedict
Benito
Benjamin
Benjy
Bennet
Bennett
Benny

Benson
Benthey
Bentley
Benton
Benvolio
Berdwell
Berecraft
Berenger
Beresford
Berg
Bergen
Berger
Bergren
Beriszl
Berk
Berkeley
Berkhead
Berkly
Bernard
Bernardo
Bernewelt
Bernie
Berny
Berowne
Berrigan
Berry
Bersh
Bert
Berthold
Bertie
Bertram
Bertreem

Berwick
Berwyn
Besnik
Best
Bettsthorne
Beval
Bevan
Beverly
Bevis
Bewforest
Bewley
Bexley
Beyers
Bhagirath
Bharat
Bhaskar
Bhavesh
Bhavin
Bhavya
Bhim
Bhima
Bhishma
Bhrigu
Bhudev
Bhupen
Bhupendra
Bhuvan
Bialy
Bigley
Bilal
Bill
Billing

Billingford
Billy
Bing
Bingham
Binyamin
Biondello
Birch
Bird
Bishop
Bishopson
Bishoptree
Bitalo
Bjorn
Blacknall
Blackwell
Blade
Bladewell
Blaine
Blair
Blaise
Blake
Blakeley
Blaxland
Blaxton
Blaz
Bledig
Blennerhayset
Blexham
Blodwell
Bloom
Blount
Blundell

Blythe	Bosley	Bradley
Bo	Bost	Bradshawe
Boa	Bostock	Bradstone
Boaz	Boston	Bradwell
Bob	Boswell	Brady
Bobbie	Bosworth	Brae
Bobby	Botan	Brahnan
Bod	Bothy	Bram
Boddenham	Botond	Bramfield
Boden	Botteler	Brampton
Bodo	Bottom	Bramwell
Bodor	Boulder	Bran
Bogart	Boult	Branch
Bogdan	Bourke	Brand
Bohan	Bourne	Brandeis
Bolton	Boville	Brander
Bonamy	Bowcer	Brandon
Bonar	Bowen	Branko
Bond	Bowett	Brant
Bonner	Bowie	Branwhaite
Booker	Bowman	Brassie
Boone	Bownell	Braunstone
Boote	Bowyar	Braxton
Booth	Boyce	Bray
Boothe	Boyd	Brayden
Borachio	Boyden	Brayles
Borden	Boyet	Braz
Borg	Brabantio	Brazil
Boris	Brad	Brecknock
Borrell	Bradbridge	Brecon
Borrow	Braden	Bredham
Bosby	Bradford	Brencis

Brendan	Brom	Burdon
Brennan	Brome	Burgess
Brent	Bromley	Burgh
Breok	Bronson	Burghill
Breton	Brook	Burgoyne
Brett	Brooke	Burhan
Brewiss	Brougham	Burian
Brewster	Broughton	Burington
Briac	Browett	Burke
Brian	Brown	Burl
Briand	Brownflet	Burle
Brice	Browning	Burley
Bridgeman	Bruce	Burlton
Briggs	Brudenell	Burnaby
Brigham	Bruno	Burnard
Brighton	Brutus	Burne
Brij	Bryan	Burnell
Brijesh	Bryant	Burnet
Brinkhurst	Bryce	Burney
Brinley	Brychan	Burnu
Brishen	Bryn	Burnum
Bristol	Brynmor	Burr
Bristow	Buck	Burt
Brock	Buckingham	Burton
Brocksby	Buckley	Busby
Broderick	Bud	Bushbury
Brodeway	Buddy	Buslingthorpe
Brodie	Budi	Buster
Brodnax	Buford	Butler
Brodny	Bulkeley	Byfield
Brody	Bulstrode	Byford
Brokehill	Burchard	Bylent

Byng
Byron

"C"

Cable
Cadby
Cadell
Cadeo
Cadman
Cadmus
Cadogan
Caedmon
Caerwyn
Caesar
Cahil
Cailan
Cailean
Cain
Caine
Caithness
Caius
Cajan
Cal
Calder
Caldwell
Caleb
Caley
Calhoun

Caliban
Calisto
Calixto
Callis
Callthorpe
Calum
Calvert
Calvin
Calvine
Cam
Camden
Cameron
Camille
Camillo
Camlin
Campbell
Campden
Candan
Candidius
Cane
Canice
Cannon
Canon
Cantilupe
Canute
Capers
Caphis
Capucius
Capulet
Caradoc
Carbonall
Carden

Cardew
Cardiff
Carel
Carew
Carey
Carl
Carleton
Carlin
Carlisle
Carlo
Carlos
Carlton
Carlyle
Carlyon
Carmelo
Carne
Carnelian
Carr
Carrick
Carrington
Carroll
Carson
Carsten
Carsyn
Carter
Carvell
Carver
Carwyn
Cary
Case
Casey
Casimir

Caspar
Casper
Cassidy
Cassio
Cassius
Cassy
Castel
Castell
Castletown
Catesby
Cathal
Cathan
Cathmor
Cato
Caton
Cavan
Cavell
Caxton
Cayden
Ceasar
Cecil
Cedric
Cely
Cemal
Cengis
Cerimon
Cesar
Chad
Chadwick
Chahaya
Chaika
Chaim

Chal
Chale
Challis
Chalmers
Chaman
Chamberlain
Champneys
Chan
Chance
Chanceller
Chancellor
Chancey
Chandan
Chander
Chandler
Chandra
Chane
Chaney
Channing
Chapal
Chapin
Chapman
Charan
Charlie
Charles
Charley
Charleton
Charlton
Chas
Chase
Chata
Chatillon

Chatwyn
Chaucer
Chauncey
Chayton
Cheddar
Chelsey
Chen
Cheney
Chernock
Cherokee
Chester
Chet
Chetan
Chetwin
Chetwood
Chevalier
Cheverell
Chevy
Cheyenne
Cheyne
Cheyney
Chiamaka
Chichester
Chico
Chike
Chilton
Chin
Chinmay
Chintu
Chiranjeev
Chiron
Chowne

Chrirag	Claus	Cobden
Chris	Clavell	Cobham
Christian	Clay	Cobley
Christie	Claybrook	Cobweb
Christmas	Clayland	Cockayne
Christopher	Clayton	Coddington
Christos	Cleary	Cody
Christy	Cledwyn	Coffin
Chrysander	Clem	Coggshall
Chuck	Clemens	Cohn
Chuckie	Clement	Colbert
Chudderley	Clem	Colby
Chung	Cleon	Cole
Church	Cleve	Coleman
Churchill	Cleveland	Colin
Churmond	Cliff	Colkins
Cian	Clifford	Collard
Ciaran	Clifton	Collin
Cicero	Clint	Colman
Ciceron	Clinton	Colmer
Ciel	Clintyn	Colon
Ciprian	Clitherow	Colt
Ciprien	Clitus	Colthurst
Ciro	Clive	Coltin
Clachas	Clopton	Colton
Clancy	Cloten	Columba
Clarence	Clovis	Coman
Clark	Clunes	Comfort
Clarke	Clyde	Cominius
Claude	Coalan	Complin
Claudio	Cobar	Compton
Claudius	Cobb	Conall

Conan	Corwin	Cristemas
Condon	Cory	Cristian
Conlan	Cosmo	Cristiano
Conley	Cossington	Cristo
Conn	Costard	Crocker
Conner	Cosworth	Cromwell
Connley	Cotton	Cronan
Connor	Coty	Crosby
Conor	Court	Crugg
Conquest	Courtenay	Csaba
Conrad	Courtland	Cseke
Conrade	Courtney	Csenger
Conroy	Covert	Csepel
Constantine	Cowill	Csombor
Conway	Cox	Csongor
Cooke	Craig	Ctirad
Cooper	Crandon	Cuba
Coorain	Crane	Cubert
Coorthopp	Cranford	Cuddon
Coppinger	Cranley	Cullen
Corban	Cranmer	Culpepper
Corbett	Cranog	Cunningham
Corby	Crawford	Cupid
Corcoran	Crawley	Curan
Cordell	Creighton	Curio
Corey	Cressy	Curnow
Corin	Crewe	Curran
Cormac	Crickett	Currier
Cornelian	Cripps	Curry
Cornelius	Crisiant	Curt
Cornell	Crisp	Curtis
Cort	Crispin	Curzon

Cuthbert
Cutler
Cutter
Cy
Cymbeline
Cynfor
Cynric
Cyprian
Cyrano
Cyric
Cyril
Cyrus

"D"

Dabert
Dacey
Dade
Dafydd
Dag
Dagan
Dagobert
Dagworth
Dahana
Dai
Dail
Dakarai
Dakota
Dakshesh

Daku
Dalbert
Dale
Daley
Dalingridge
Dallas
Dallin
Dalton
Daly
Dalziel
Damek
Damen
Damian
Damien
Damodar
Damon
Damsell
Dan
Dana
Danby
Dane
Danett
Daniel
Daniel / Dan
Danior
Dannie
Danny
Dante
Danvers
Dara
Darby
Darcy

Darel
Daren
Darien
Darin
Darius
Darley
Darnell
Darrel
Darrell
Darren
Darryl
Darshan
Dartagnan
Darthmouth
Darton
Daruka
Darwin
Daryl
Dattatreya
Daubernon
Daunce
Dauncey
Daundelyon
Dave
Davey
David
Davidson
Davie
Davin
Davis
Davy
Dawa

Dawne	Demitrius	Derry
Day	Demos	Derward
Dayton	Dempe	Derwent
Deacon	Dempsey	Derwin
Deacons	Dempster	Derwood
Dean	Demyan	Derwyn
Decker	Denby	Des
Declan	Dencourt	Desford
Decretas	Denes	Desiderio
Dedric	Denham	Desiderius
Dedrick	Denholm	Desmond
Deepak	Denis	Dev
Deering	Deniz	Devang
Deiphobus	Denley	Devante
Del	Dennis	Devarsi
Delabere	Dennison	Devdan
Delamere	Denton	Deverell
Delaney	Denver	Devereux
Delano	Denzel	Devesh
Delbert	Denzil	Devi
Deli	Deo	Devin
Dell	Derain	Devitri
Delling	Derby	Devlin
Delly	Derek	Devon
Delmar	Derex	Devrity
Delmore	Dericott	Dewey
Delroy	Derington	Dewi
Delsin	Dermot	Dewitt
Delwyn	Derrell	Dexter
Deman	Derren	Dhananjay
Demas	Derrick	Dharma
Demetrius	Derron	Dharmavira

Dharmendra
Dharmesh
Dharuna
Dhatri
Dhaval
Dheran
Dhruv
Diamond
Dian
Diarmad
Diarmid
Dick
Dickie
Dickinson
Dickson
Dicky
Didier
Diederik
Diego
Dieter
Dietrich
Digby
Diggory
Dilip
Dillon
Dimitri
Dimmock
Dinesh
Dinkar
Dinley
Dino
Dinsdale

Diomedes
Dion
Dione
Dionysus
Dirk
Dirke
Divyesh
Dixon
Dixton
Djavan
Dmitri
Dobry
Dodd
Doddle
Dogberry
Dogmersfield
Dolabella
Dolan
Dolf
Dolph
Dominic
Dominick
Domokos
Don
Donahue
Donalbain
Donald
Donatien
Donato
Donegal
Donnelly
Donnett

Donnie
Donny
Donoghue
Donohue
Donovan
Dooley
Dorak
Doran
Doreward
Dorian
Dorjee
Dormer
Doron
Dorset
Dory
Doug
Dougal
Douglas
Douglass
Dov
Dove
Dover
Dow
Doyle
Dragan
Drake
Draper
Draw
Drayton
Drew
Driscoll
Dromio

Drostan
Druce
Drury
Dryden
Dryland
Drystan
Duane
Duarte
Dudley
Duff
Dugal
Dugald
Dugan
Duglas
Duke
Dull
Dumaine
Duman
Dunbar
Duncan
Dunch
Duncombe
Dunham
Dunley
Dunmore
Dunn
Dunstan
Dural
Durand
Duranjaya
Durant
Durdanius

Duredent
Durham
Durjaya
Durmada
Durriken
Durward
Durwin
Dusan
Dusteby
Dustin
Dutch
Dvimidha
Dwaine
Dwane
Dwayne
Dwennon
Dwight
Dyami
Dye
Dyfan
Dylan
Dymas
Dynham
Dyre

"E"

Eachan
Eamnonn

Eamon
Earl
Earnest
Earvin
Eaton
Eban
Ebenezer
Eberhard
Ebrahim
Ed
Edan
Edbert
Eddie
Eddy
Eden
Edgar
Edgardo
Edgcombe
Edgerton
Edison
Edlin
Edmond
Edmund
Edolf
Edom
Edric
Edsel
Edward
Edwardo
Edwards
Edwin
Efrain

Efram	Eldon	Elsdon
Efrem	Eldred	Elston
Egan	Eldric	Elton
Egbert	Eldrich	Elu
Egerton	Eldridge	Elvin
Egeus	Eldwin	Elvis
Eggerley	Eleazar	Elvy
Egil	Elek	Elward
Eglamour	Elezar	Elwin
Eglisfeld	Elgan	Elwood
Egmont	Elgar	Ely
Egon	Eli	Emerson
Egor	Elia	Emery
Egyed	Elias	Emil
Ehner	Elijah	Emilio
Ehno	Eliot	Emir
Ehnore	Elisha	Emlen
Ehren	Emmett	Emlyn
Ehud	Elkan	Emmanuel
Eideard	Ellar	Emmet
Einar	Ellard	Emrey
Eirik	Ellery	Emrick
Eisig	Elliot	Emrys
Ekachakra	Elliott	Emyr
Eknath	Ellis	Enda
Eladio	Ellison	Endymion
Elan	Elmar	Eneas
Eland	Elmebrigge	Engelbert
Elbert	Elmo	Engham
Elbow	Elner	Engleford
Elden	Eloy	Englisch
Eldin	Elroy	Ennis

Ennor
Enoch
Enos
Enrico
Enrique
Enzo
Eoin
Ephraim
Epworth
Erasmus
Erastus
Ercole
Erebus
Erek
Erewaker
Erhard
Eric
Erik
Erin
Erith
Erland
Ermanno
Ermin
Ernest
Ernie
Eros
Errol
Erroll
Erskine
Ertham
Eruera
Ervin

Erwin
Eryx
Esau
Esbern
Escalus
Escanes
Esidor
Esmond
Esmund
Esra
Essex
Essien
Estbury
Este
Esteban
Estes
Eston
Etchingham
Ethan
Ethelred
Etienne
Eton
Etton
Ettore
Etzel
Euan
Eudor
Eugene
Eumann
Euridice
Eurwyn
Eusebio

Eustace
Evan
Evander
Evangelos
Evelyn
Everard
Everdon
Everet
Everett
Everild
Everley
Evingar
Evzen
Ewald
Ewan
Ewart
Ewing
Eyan
Eydie
Eyer
Eyston
Ezekiel
Ezio
Ezra

"F"

Faber
Fabian

Fabrice	Fayneman	Fiachra
Fabron	Faysal	Fidel
Fadil	Fear	Fielding
Fagan	Februus	Fienley
Fairfax	Fedele	Fife
Fairley	Federico	Figaro
Faisal	Felbrigg	Filbert
Faldo	Feld	Filip
Falgun	Felipe	Filippo
Falk	Felix	Finbar
Falkner	Felton	Finch
Fallon	Fenn	Findern
Fane	Fenton	Fineas
Faraji	Fenwick	Fineux
Farand	Feodore	Fingal
Farid	Ferdinand	Finian
Fariel	Ferenc	Finlay
Farindon	Fergal	Finley
Farkas	Fergus	Finn
Farley	Ferguson	Finnegan
Farman	Fernando	Fionn
Farnell	Fernleigh	Firdos
Farnley	Fernley	Firmin
Farook	Feroz	Firth
Farquhar	Ferran	Fisher
Farrar	Ferrand	Fisk
Farrell	Ferrer	Fitch
Farriss	Ferris	Fitton
Faulkner	Feste	Fitz
Faust	Festus	Fitzgeoffrey
Favian	Feversham	Fitzgerald
Faxon	Ffionn	Fitzherbert

Fitzhugh	Foliot	Frasier
Fitzjames	Foljambe	Fraunces
Fitzlewis	Folkus	Frayne
Fitzpatrick	Follon	Fred
Fitzralph	Follywolle	Freddie
Fitzroy	Folsham	Freddy
Fitzwarren	Fonteyn	Frederick
Fitzwilliam	Fonz	Free
Fjodor	Fonzie	Freeman
Flannan	Forbes	Freen
Flannery	Ford	Freer
Flavian	Forder	Fremont
Flavius	Forest	Freville
Fleance	Forester	Frewell
Fleet	Forrest	Frigyes
Fleeting	Forrester	Frilende
Fleetwood	Forster	Frilleck
Fleming	Fortescue	Frith
Fletcher	Fortey	Fritz
Flexney	Fortinbras	Froggenhall
Flint	Fortunato	Fromond
Floke	Foster	Froste
Florian	Fowler	Froth
Floritzel	Fox	Frowseloure
Flower	Francey	Frye
Floyd	Francis	Fudo
Fluellen	Francisco	Fujita
Flynn	Frank	Fulbright
Fodd	Franklin	Fulburne
Fodor	Frans	Fulke
Fogg	Franz	Fuller
Folant	Fraser	Fulmer

Fulton
Furnace
Furnell
Fyfe
Fyodor

"G"

Gabai
Gable
Gabor
Gabriel
Gabe
Gadiel
Gadil
Gafna
Gagan
Gage
Gainsford
Gair
Gaius
Galahad
Gale
Galen
Galeno
Galey
Galip
Gallagher
Gallard
Galloway
Gallus

Galor
Galton
Galvin
Galway
Gamal
Gamaliel
Gaman
Gamba
Gamble
Gamel
Ganan
Gandolf
Ganesh
Gannon
Ganymede
Gara
Gardiner
Gardner
Gare
Gareth
Garett
Garfield
Garin
Garland
Garman
Garmond
Garner
Garnet
Garnis
Garrard
Garret
Garrett

Garrick
Garridan
Garrison
Garron
Garry
Garth
Garton
Garvey
Garvin
Garwood
Gary
Garyson
Gascoigne
Gaspar
Gasper
Gassy
Gaston
Gaurav
Gautam
Gautama
Gautier
Gavan
Gavell
Gavin
Gavrie
Gavril
Gawain
Gayle
Gaylord
Geary
Gedding
Gedeon

Geert	Gibbs	Glen
Geet	Gibson	Glendon
Geir	Gideon	Glenn
Gelar	Gifford	Glennon
Gene	Gilbert	Glover
Genesis	Gil	Glyn
Geoff	Gilby	Glynn
Geoffrey	Gilchrist	Gobberd
Geordi	Giles	Goddam
Geordie	Gilford	Goddard
George	Gill	Godfrey
Gerad	Gillespie	Godwin
Geraint	Gillet	Gold
Gerald	Gilmer	Golding
Gerard	Gilroy	Goldwell
Gerik	Gino	Goliath
Germain	Ginter	Gomer
Gerome	Ginton	Gomershall
Geronimo	Giordano	Gomez
Gerry	Giovanni	Gomfrey
Gershom	Giraldo	Gonson
Gervase	Girish	Gonzalo
Gerville	Girra	Good
Gerwyn	Girvan	Goodenouth
Gerzson	Gisborne	Gooder
Geste	Gittens	Goodluck
Gethin	Giulio	Goodnestone
Ghassan	Giuseppe	Goodrick
Gi	Givon	Goodrington
Giacobbe	Gladstone	Goodwin
Giacomo	Gladwin	Gopal
Gianni	Glanville	Gordon

Gordy
Gore
Goring
Gorman
Gorney
Goronwy
Gorran
Gorst
Gosebourne
Gottfried
Gough
Govinda
Gower
Grady
Graeme
Grafton
Graham
Granger
Grant
Grantham
Granville
Gratian
Gratiano
Gray
Grayson
Greene
Greenway
Greg
Greger
Gregg
Gregory
Gremio

Grenefeld
Gresham
Greville
Grey
Griffin
Griffith
Grimbald
Griswold
Grobbam
Grofhurst
Groston
Grosvenor
Grove
Grover
Grumio
Gryffyn
Gugliehno
Guiderius
Guido
Guildenstern
Guildford
Guillaume
Guillermo
Gul
Gulab
Gunnar
Gunther
Guntur
Gurion
Gurkan
Gus
Gustav

Guthrie
Guy
Gwilym
Gwyn
Gwynfor
Gye
Gyles
Gyula

"H"

Habib
Hackett
Hackman
Hadar
Hadden
Haddock
Haddon
Hadi
Hadley
Hadresham
Hadrian
Hadwin
Hafiz
Hagan
Hagen
Hagley
Hahn
Haig
Haile
Haines

Hakan	Hammond	Haresh
Hakebourne	Hamon	Harewell
Hakim	Hampden	Harford
Hakon	Hampton	Hargreave
Hal	Hanan	Hargreve
Halbert	Hancock	Hari
Halden	Handel	Harish
Haldor	Ha-Neul	Harith
Hale	Hanford	Harlakinden
Haley	Hani	Harlan
Halford	Hank	Harland
Halian	Hanke	Harleigh
Halifax	Hanley	Harleston
Halil	Hannes	Harley
Hall	Hannibal	Harlow
Hallam	Hannu	Harman
Halley	Hans	Harold
Halse	Hansart	Haroun
Halsey	Hansel	Harpeden
Halstead	Hansi	Harper
Halsten	Hanson	Harris
Halton	Haral	Harrison
Halvard	Harald	Harry
Hamal	Harbird	Harsh
Hamar	Harbottle	Hart
Hambard	Harcourt	Harte
Hamid	Harden	Hartley
Hamilton	Hardik	Hartman
Hamish	Harding	Hartwell
Hamlet	Hardwin	Hartwin
Hamlin	Hardy	Hartwood
Hammer	Hare	Haru

Harun	Heathcliff	Herbert
Harvard	Heathcote	Hercules
Harvey	Hecate	Herleston
Harwin	Hector	Herman
Harwood	Heddwyn	Hermes
Hasad	Hedley	Hermon
Hasard	Heilyn	Hernando
Hasim	Heinrich	Herold
Haslett	Heinz	Heron
Hassan	Helaku	Herrick
Hastin	Helenus	Hershel
Hastings	Helicanus	Herst
Hatch	Heller	Hertcomb
Hatcliff	Helm	Hertford
Hautreeve	Helmut	Herve
Havelock	Helmuth	Hervey
Haven	Hemal	Herwin
Havika	Hemang	Hesketh
Hawkins	Hemant	Hew
Hawksworth	Hemendra	Hewett
Hawley	Hemi	Hewie
Hawtrey	Henderson	Hewston
Hayden	Hendra	Heydon
Haye	Hendy	Heyward
Hayes	Henleigh	Heywood
Hayton	Henley	Heyworth
Hayward	Henning	Hiatt
Haywood	Henri	Hieronymus
Hazlett	Henrik	Higden
Hazlitt	Henry	Highgate
Hearst	Henshawe	Hilary
Heath	Herb	Hildebrand

Hilderley
Hill
Hillel
Hilton
Hinson
Hippolyte
Hiram
Hiroshi
Hirsh
Hitchcock
Hiten
Hitendra
Hitesh
Ho
Hoare
Hobart
Hodgson
Hogan
Holbrook
Holcott
Holden
Holger
Holgernes
Holland
Hollis
Holman
Holmes
Holofernes
Holsey
Holt
Holton
Homer

Hont
Hopkin
Hopton
Horace
Horatio
Hori
Horman
Hornebolt
Hornley
Horsey
Horst
Hortensio
Hortensius
Horthall
Horton
Hosea
Hosteler
Hotham
Houghton
Houston
Howard
Howe
Howell
Howie
Hridayesh
Hrishikesh
Hsin
Huatare
Huba
Hubert
Huddleston
Hudson

Huey
Hugeford
Hugh
Hughes
Hugo
Humbert
Hume
Humphrey
Hungate
Hunor
Hunter
Huntley
Huon
Hurst
Hussain
Hussein
Hussey
Hutchinson
Hutton
Huw
Huxley
Hyam
Hyatt
Hyde
Hylton
Hymen
Hyram
Hywel

"I"

Iachima
Iagan
Iago
Iain
Ian
Ibeamaka
Ibrahim
Icarus
Ichabod
Iden
Idris
Idwal
Iestin
Iestyn
Ieuan
Ifor
Ignacio
Ignatius
Igor
Ihorangi
Ike
Ikey
Ilar
Ilario
Ilhan
Ilias
Ilie
Ilya
Imam

Immanuel
Imre
Ince
Indra
Ingemar
Inger
Inglebert
Ingmar
Ingo
Ingolf
Ingram
Inigo
Innes
Innocent
Inwood
Ioannes
Iolo
Iolyn
Ion
Iorweth
Ira
Iravan
Irawaru
Irvin
Irving
Irwin
Isa
Isaac
Isaiah
Isha
Ishmael
Ishver

Isidore
Isidro
Isley
Israel
Istvan
Itzaak
Itzak
Itziamar
Itzik
Ivan
Ivar
Ives
Ivo
Ivor
Izaak

"J"

Jabari
Jabez
Jabir
Jace
Jacek
Jack
Jack
Jackmann
Jackson
Jacob
Jacques
Jacy

Jaedon	Jarlath	Jeffrey
Jael	Jarman	Jehosophat
Jafar	Jaron	Jelani
Jagdish	Jaroslav	Jendring
Jagger	Jarrad	Jenkins
Jago	Jarrah	Jenney
Jaiden	Jarratt	Jens
Jaidev	Jarred	Jensen
Jaidon	Jarrod	Jeptha
Jaime	Jarvis	Jerald
Jake	Jaryn	Jerara
Jakob	Jason	Jered
Jakub	Jasper	Jeremiah
Jal	Jatin	Jeremias
Jaleel	Java	Jeremy
Jalen	Javan	Jeri
Jalil	Javed	Jericho
Jamal	Javier	Jermain
James	Jay	Jermyn
Jamie	Jayant	Jerod
Jamieson	Jayden	Jerold
Jamison	Jaysukh	Jerolin
Jan	Jayvyn	Jerome
Janak	Jean	Jerrard
Janardan	Jed	Jerrie
Janner	Jedd	Jerry
Janus	Jedediah	Jervaise
Japhet	Jedidiah	Jervis
Jaques	Jedrek	Jerzy
Jared	Jeevan	Jesse
Jarek	Jeff	Jesus
Jarel	Jefferson	Jet

Jethro
Jetmir
Jibril
Jiger
Jilesh
Jim
Jimmie
Jimmy
Jimuta
Jin
Jinesh
Jiri
Jiro
Jirra
Jiten
Jitender
Jitendra
Jivana
Jivin
Jo
Joab
Joachim
Joakim
Job
Jocelin
Jock
Jody
Joe
Joel
Joey
Joh
Johann

Johannes
John
John Paul
John Wesley
Johnny
Johnson
Jolyon
Jon
Jonah
Jonathan
Jonny
Joo-Chan
Joost
Joram
Jordan
Jorge
Jorgen
Jorma
Jory
Jose
Josef
Joseph
Josephus
Joshua
Josiah
Joslin
Joss
Joulon
Jourdain
Jourdan
Jove
Jowan

Jowchet
Jozef
Jozsef
Juan
Judah
Judd
Jude
Julian
Julius
Juma
Jung
Junior
Junius
Jurgen
Justin
Justus
Jyotis

"K"

Kabir
Kabos
Kada
Kadin
Kadir
Kadosa
Kahn
Kahoku
Kai
Kaikara

Kailash	Kardos	Kearney
Kain	Karel	Keary
Kalani	Kari	Keaton
Kalb	Karim	Keckilpenny
Kalden	Karl	Kedar
Kale	Karma	Keefe
Kaleb	Karol	Keegan
Kaleo	Karsa	Keeland
Kalid	Karsten	Keeley
Kalidas	Kartal	Keenan
Kalil	Kartik	Keeran
Kalkin	Kartikeya	Kees
Kalman	Kasch	Kegan
Kalpanath	Kasen	Keir
Kalti	Kasey	Keiran
Kama	Kasim	Keith
Kamadev	Kasimir	Kelan
Kamal	Kaspar	Kelby
Kami	Kasper	Keled
Kamil	Kateb	Keleman
Kamlesh	Kathel	Kell
Kanak	Kauri	Kellen
Kanan	Kaushal	Keller
Kanaye	Kaushik	Kellett
Kane	Kavan	Kelly
Kaniel	Kavi	Kelsey
Kano	Kay	Kelso
Kapil	Kayin	Kelt
Kaplony	Kayne	Kelvin
Kapolcs	Kazimir	Kemal
Karan	Kean	Kembell
Kardal	Keane	Kemble

Kemenes	Kermit	Killingworth
Kemp	Kern	Kim
Ken	Kernick	Kimball
Kenan	Kernow	Kimberley
Kendall	Kerr	Kin
Kende	Kerrin	King
Kendra	Kerry	Kinga
Kendrick	Kers	Kinge
Kenelm	Kersen	Kingsley
Kenley	Kerwin	Kingston
Kenn	Keshav	Kinnard
Kennard	Kester	Kinnel
Kennedy	Kesteven	Kinsey
Kenneth	Ketan	Kintan
Kenny	Keve	Kipling
Kenrich	Keverne	Kipp
Kenrick	Kevin	Kiran
Kent	Key	Kirby
Kenton	Keyon	Kirill
Kenver	Khairi	Kirit
Kenward	Khalid	Kirk
Kenwyn	Khalif	Kirkeby
Kenya	Khalil	Kirkley
Kenyon	Khorshed	Kirkwood
Keon	Khortdad	Kiron
Keona	Khoury	Kirwin
Keoni	Kidwelly	Kisho
Ker	Kiefer	Kishore
Kerby	Kieran	Kit
Kerecsen	Killara	Kito
Kereteki	Killian	Kitson
Keriell	Killigrew	Kitto

Kiva	Kottow	**"L"**
Kiyoshi	Kovan	
Klaas	Kozma	Laban
Klaes	Kripa	Label
Klaud	Kris	Laborc
Klaus	Krischnan	Lachlan
Klea	Krishna	Lacy
Klemens	Krispen	Ladd
Kliment	Krispin	Ladislav
Knighton	Kristen	Ladomar
Knivetton	Kristian	Lae
Knody	Kristoffer	Laertes
Knox	Krunal	Lafayette
Knoyll	Kulan	Lafe
Knut	Kuldeep	Lafeu
Knyvett	Kulvir	Lai
Kolet	Kumar	Laibrook
Kolos	Kunal	Laidley
Kolya	Kund	Laird
Konan	Kupe	Lakota
Konol	Kurt	Lakshman
Konrad	Kuruk	Lakshya
Konstantin	Kusagra	Lalit
Kont	Kush	Lam
Kontar	Kushan	Laman
Koora	Kwan	Lamar
Koorong	Kyle	Lambert
Korey	Kyler	Lamberto
Kornel	Kynan	Lambton
Korvin	Kyne	Lamech
Kosmo	Kyran	Lamont
Kostya		

Lance	Laughlin	Leigh
Lancelot	Launce	Leighlin
Lander	Launceleyn	Leighton
Landers	Launcelot	Leith
Landon	Laurence	Lel
Lane	Laurie	Leland
Lang	Lavache	Leman
Langford	Lave	Lemuel
Langley	Lawford	Len
Langston	Lawler	Lennie
Langworth	Lawley	Lennon
Lani	Lawnder	Lennox
Lann	Lawrance	Lenny
Lanny	Lawrence	Lensar
Lantos	Lawson	Lenton
Lanyon	Lawton	Leo
Laoghaire	Laxman	Leon
Lappage	Layland	Leonard
Laris	Layton	Leonardo
Larrie	Lazarus	Leonato
Larry	le Bone	Leonidas
Lars	Leal	Leonine
Larson	Leander	Leontes
Lartius	Lear	Leopold
Lascelles	LeBeau	Leron
Lasse	Lech	Leroy
Laszlo	Lee	Les
Latham	Leech	Leshem
Latif	Leeds	Lesley
Latimer	Lehel	Leslie
Latton	Lehenard	Lesta
Lauchlan	Leif	Lester

Lestrange	Linley	Lond
Letterford	Linton	London
Lev	Linus	Long
Levent	Linwood	Longaville
Levente	Lionel	Longton
Leventhorpe	Lipet	Lonnie
Leverer	Liripine	Lorand
Leverett	Lisle	Lorant
Leverton	Litchfield	Loren
Leveson	Litcott	Lorenz
Levi	Littlebury	Lorenzo
Levin	Litton	Lorimer
Lewie	Liverich	Lorin
Lewis	Livesey	Lorinc
Lex	Livingston	Loring
Leyman	Ljluka	Lorne
Leynham	Llewellyn	Lothair
Leynthall	Llfryn	Lothar
Li	Lloyd	Lothario
Liall	Lobsang	Loughlin
Liam	Loch	Louis
Lief	Locke	Lovel
Limsey	Lockton	Lovell
Lincoln	Lockwood	Loveney
Lind	Loddington	Lowan
Lindan	Lodovico	Lowell
Lindberg	Logan	Lowth
Lindell	Lokesh	Loxley
Linden	Loman	Loyal
Lindley	Lombard	Luc
Lindsay	Lome	Lucas
Linford	Lon	Lucentio

Lucian
Lucilius
Lucio
Lucius
Lucretius
Lucullus
Lucy
Ludlow
Ludovic
Ludsthorp
Ludvig
Ludwig
Ludwik
Luigi
Luis
Luke
Lumbard
Lundy
Lunt
Lupton
Luther
Luzio
Lyfeld
Lykaios
Lyle
Lyman
Lymoges
Lyn
Lyndell
Lyndon
Lynn
Lyon

Lyonel
Lyre
Lysander
Lysimachus
Lytton

"M"

Maaka
Maarten
Mablevi
Mabon
Mac
Macarius
Macbeth
Macdonald
Macduff
Mace
Macey
Mackay
Mackenzie
Macmorris
Macon
Macy
Madan
Maddock
Maddox
Madhav
Madhusudhana
Madison
Madoc

Madron
Magee
Magne
Magnus
Magus
Mahabala
Mahavira
Mahendra
Mahesh
Mahir
Mahmood
Mahomet
Mahon
Maitland
Maitreya
Majid
Major
Maka
Makani
Makepeace
Makepiece
Makis
Mako
Maksim
Makya
Mal
Malachi
Malcolm
Malcom
Malden
Malemayns
Malik

Malin	Mansoor	Marland
Malins	Manston	Marley
Malise	Mansukh	Marlon
Mallee	Mansur	Marlow
Mallory	Manu	Marmaduke
Malone	Manuel	Marmion
Malster	Manus	Maron
Maltoun	Mapilton	Marot
Malvern	Marama	Marris
Malvolio	Marc	Marron
Mamillius	Marcade	Marsden
Mamoru	Marcel	Marsh
Manavendra	Marcell	Marshall
Manchu	Marcello	Marsham
Manco	Marcellus	Marston
Mandek	Marcheford	Marten
Mandel	Marcin	Martin
Mander	Marco	Martius
Mandhatri	Marcos	Marty
Mandu	Marcus	Marvin
Manfield	Marden	Marvyn
Manfred	Mardian	Masa
Mani	Margarelon	Masakazu
Manik	Marian	Masheck
Manish	Marijan	Maslin
Manley	Marino	Mason
Mannie	Mario	Massimo
Manning	Marion	Massingberd
Mannix	Marius	Masud
Manny	Mark	Matai
Manoj	Markandeya	Matanga
Mansa	Markeley	Matareka

Matari
Mather
Mathias
Matt
Matthew
Maudit
Maui
Mauntell
Maurice
Mawgan
Max
Maxey
Maximilian
Maxwell
Maycott
Maydestone
Mayer
Maynard
Mayne
Maynwaring
Mayon
Mead
Meara
Mearann
Mecaenus
Medeley
Medord
Medwin
Megyer
Mehetabel
Mehul
Meir

Meirion
Meka
Mel
Melancton
Melbourne
Melburn
Melchior
Melford
Melik
Melor
Melrose
Melun
Melville
Melvin
Melvyn
Menachem
Menadue
Menas
Mendel
Menecrates
Menelaus
Menenius
Menteith
Menyhart
Mercade
Mercer
Mercutio
Merden
Meredith
Mereworth
Meriwether
Merle

Merlin
Merrick
Merrill
Merryn
Merstun
Mert
Merten
Merton
Merv
Mervin
Mervyn
Messala
Metcalf
Mete
Meyer
Mica
Micah
Micajah
Michael
Michelangelo
Michelgrove
Mick
Mickey
Midas
Middleton
Miguel
Mihaly
Mihir
Mikael
Mike
Mikhail
Miki

Mikkel	Mitali	Montmorency
Mikkeli	Mitch	Monty
Mikko	Mitcham	Moore
Miklos	Mitchel	Mopsa
Miko	Mitchell	Mor
Miksa	Mitesh	Moray
Milan	Mladen	Morcum
Milbourn	Moffatt	Mordecai
Milburn	Mog	Mordred
Miles	Mogens	More
Milford	Mogo	Morecott
Milind	Mohammed	Morgan
Mill	Mohan	Moriarty
Millard	Mohin	Morice
Miller	Mohinder	Moritz
Millet	Mohit	Morland
Millis	Moland	Morley
Milner	Molins	Morrell
Milo	Molloy	Morrie
Milos	Molyngton	Morris
Milsent	Monde	Morrison
Milton	Monro	Morry
Minar	Monroe	Morse
Minas	Montacute	Mort
Miner	Montagu	Morten
Minesh	Montague	Mortimer
Ming	Montana	Morton
Mingma	Montano	Morty
Minos	Monte	Morven
Miro	Montego	Moryet
Miroslav	Montgomery	Moses
Mischa	Monti	Moshe

Mosi
Moss
Mostyn
Motega
Motesfont
Moth
Mountjoy
Mowan
Mowfurth
Mubarak
Mugg
Muhammad
Muir
Mukasa
Mukhtar
Mukta
Mukul
Mukunda
Mulga
Mull
Mullens
Mullion
Mumtaz
Mungo
Munro
Murdoch
Murdock
Murphy
Murray
Musa
Mustafa
Mustardseed

Muston
Mutius
Muzaffer
Myall
Myer
Myles
Mylo
Mylor
Myron

"N"

Naaman
Nabendu
Nabil
Nabulung
Nachiketa
Nachmanke
Nadav
Nadir
Naeem
Nahum
Naimish
Nairn
Nakul
Nalong
Nalren
Nambur
Namdev

Namid
Namir
Nanda
Nandin
Nandor
Nantan
Napoleon
Narayan
Narayana
Narbridge
Narciso
Narcissus
Nardu
Narendra
Naresh
Narrah
Narsi
Nartana
Nash
Nasir
Nassir
Nat
Natal
Natale
Natan
Nathan
Nathaniel
Naum
Naveen
Nawang
Nayan
Neal

Neale	Newton	Nino
Ned	Newt	Nioka
Neddie	Niall	Niraj
Neddy	Nic	Niramitra
Nedim	Nicholas	Niran
Neel	Nickie	Niranjan
Neeraj	Nickson	Nirav
Nehemiah	Nicky	Nirel
Neil	Nico	Nishad
Neill	Nicodemus	Nishan
Nek	Nicol	Nisi
Nelek	Nicolas	Nitesh
Nelson	Nieander	Niven
Nemo	Niel	Nivens
Neo	Niels	Nixon
Nerang	Nieodemus	Noadiah
Nerhim	Nigel	Noah
Nero	Nihar	Noam
Neron	Nike	Noble
Nesim	Nikhil	Nodin
Nesip	Nikita	Noe
Nestor	Niklaus	Noel
Nevada	Nikunj	Noi
Nevan	Nilay	Noke
Neville	Nils	Nolan
Nevin	Nilson	Norbert
Nevinson	Nima	Norbu
Newbold	Nimai	Norbury
Newdegate	Nimbus	Norden
Newell	Nimesh	Norm
Newlyn	Nimrod	Norman
Newman	Ninian	Normand

Norris	Obadiah	Oleos
North	Obediah	Olier
Northclif	Obelix	Olin
Northrop	Oberon	Olingworth
Northwood	Obert	Oliver
Norton	Obiajulu	Olivier
Norville	Obson	Ollie
Norvin	Ochen	Omar
Norwell	Octavius	Omarjeet
Norwich	Oddvar	Ompoly
Norwood	Odell	Ond
Notfeld	Odern	Onslow
Nottingham	Odil	Onur
Nowell	Odin	Ora
Nowra	Odion	Oral
Nuncio	Odolf	Orad
Nur	Odon	Oram
Nurhan	Odysseus	Oran
Nuri	Ogden	Orazio
Nye	Ogilvie	Orban
Nyek	Ogilvy	Ordway
Nyle	Oglesby	Orelious
Nym	Oguz	Oren
Nysell	Okan	Orestes
	Oke	Orfeo
	Okely	Orford
	Oken	Orion
	Okko	Orlan
"O"	Olaf	Orlando
	Olcay	Orman
Oakes	Oldrich	Ormond
Oakley	Oleg	Ormos

Oroiti
Orpheus
Orran
Orren
Orrin
Orsen
Orsino
Orson
Orton
Orville
Orvin
Osaze
Osbert
Osborn
Osborne
Oscar
Osgood
Osillbury
Osip
Oskar
Oskari
Osman
Osmar
Osmond
Osric
Ossian
Osteler
Oswald
Oswin
Oszlar
Otello
Othello

Otis
Ottavio
Otto
Otway
Outlawe
Ove
Ovid
Owen
Oxenbrigg
Oxford
Oxton
Oz
Ozan
Ozaner
Ozias
Ozor

"P"

Paavo
Pablo
Pacifico
Packard
Paco
Paddy
Padget
Padgett
Padmakar
Padraig

Padruig
Page
Pagg
Pahniro
Paige
Paine
Paki
Palani
Pallav
Palmer
Palti
Pan
Pancho
Pancras
Pancrazio
Pandarus
Pandita
Pandya
Pankaj
Panos
Panshawe
Panthino
Panyin
Paolo
Papley
Parag
Paramartha
Paras
Paris
Park
Parker
Parkin

Parlan	Peacock	Per
Parolles	Pearce	Perchehay
Parr	Peck	Percival
Parrett	Peckham	Percy
Parri	Peder	Peregrine
Parris	Pedr	Pericles
Parrish	Pedrek	Peril
Parry	Pedro	Perri
Parsefal	Pedrog	Perris
Parsifal	Peel	Perrot
Parsons	Pelin	Perry
Parth	Pell	Perryvall
Partha	Pellegrin	Perth
Pasang	Pelletoot	Pete
Pascal	Peltie	Peter
Paston	Pelton	Petham
Pat	Pemba	Petley
Patamon	Pemberton	Petroc
Patern	Pembroke	Petruchio
Patony	Penhallick	Pettit
Patrick	Penley	Pettwood
Patroclus	Penn	Peverall
Patton	Pennebrygg	Peyton
Paul	Penrice	Phelan
Paulo	Penrith	Phelps
Pavel	Penrod	Philario
Pax	Penrose	Philbert
Paxton	Pentele	Philemon
Payne	Penwyn	Philip
Payton	Pepe	Philips
Pazman	Pepin	Phillip
Peace	Pepper	Phillips

Philo	Pitney	Powys
Philostrate	Pitt	Prabhakar
Philotus	Pius	Prabodh
Phineas	Piusz	Pradeep
Phoenix	Piyush	Praful
Phuoc	Placido	Prakash
Phuong	Plato	Pramana
Picerious	Platon	Pramath
Pickford	Platt	Pramsu
Pierce	Playters	Pranav
Piero	Pleasant	Pranay
Pierpont	Plessey	Prasad
Pierre	Plimmswood	Prasanth
Pierrot	Pluto	Prasata
Piers	Poff	Prashant
Pierson	Pol	Prasoon
Piet	Pole	Prassana
Pietro	Polixenes	Pratap
Piggott	Pollock	Pratik
Pilan	Polonius	Pratt
Pinch	Polsted	Pratyush
Pindan	Polton	Praveen
Pindari	Pomeroy	Pray
Pindarus	Pompey	Prayag
Pinnock	Pongor	Preetish
Pino	Pontius	Prelate
Pinty	Porter	Prem
Pip	Portington	Prentice
Piran	Potter	Prescott
Pisanio	Powell	Presley
Pistol	Powlett	Preston
Pita	Pownder	Prewitt

Priam
Price
Primel
Primo
Prince
Prior
Prithu
Privrata
Probert
Proctor
Proculeius
Prometheus
Prophet
Prosper
Prospero
Proteus
Prowd
Pryce
Pryderi
Pryor
Ptolemy
Publius
Puck
Pulkit
Pundarik
Puranjay
Purles
Pursglove
Purujit
Purvis
Pusan
Puskara

Putnam

"Q"

Quentin
Quinn
Quartus
Quincy
Qasim
Quint

"R"

Rab
Rabbie
Rad
Radborne
Radcliff
Radcliffe
Radek
Radford
Radley
Radman
Radnor
Radom
Raeburn
Rafael

Rafe
Raffaele
Rafferty
Rafi
Rafiq
Rafu
Raghnall
Ragin
Ragnar
Rahman
Rahul
Raibeart
Raidon
Raimy
Rainer
Rainier
Raivata
Raj
Rajan
Rajanikant
Rajendra
Rajesh
Rajiv
Rakesh
Raleigh
Ralph
Ralston
Ram
Raman
Ramanuja
Rambert
Rambures

Ramelan	Rarna	Reading
Rameses	Rashid	Reagan
Ramesh	Rashne	Rearden
Ramiro	Rasmus	Reardon
Ramon	Rastus	Rebel
Rampston	Rata	Redford
Ramsay	Ratcliff	Redman
Ramsden	Ratri	Redmond
Ramsey	Raudell	Redmund
Ranald	Rauf	Reece
Rance	Raul	Reed
Rand	Raven	Reede
Randal	Ravi	Rees
Randall	Ravid	Reese
Randell	Ravindra	Reeve
Randie	Ravinger	Regan
Randolph	Rawiri	Regin
Randy	Rawley	Reginald
Ranen	Rawlin	Regis
Ranger	Rawlins	Rego
Rangi	Rawly	Rehan
Ranjan	Rawson	Reid
Ranjeet	Ray	Reilly
Ranjit	Rayburn	Reinhard
Rankin	Raymon	Reinhold
Ransford	Raymond	Remington
Ransley	Raynard	Remus
Ransom	Rayner	Remy
Rantidev	Raynold	Renaldo
Ranulf	Raynsford	Renard
Raoul	Razi	Renaud
Raphael	Read	Rendor

Rene	Rico	Roarke
Renfred	Rider	Rob
Renfrew	Ridgeway	Robbins
Rennard	Ridgley	Robert
Renny	Ridley	Robertson
Renshaw	Rigby	Robi
Reuben	Rigg	Robin
Reuel	Rikard	Robinson
Rex	Rikin	Robyn
Rey	Riley	Rocco
Reynaldo	Rimon	Rochester
Reynard	Rinaldo	Rochforth
Reynes	Ring	Rock
Reynold	Ringer	Rockley
Rezse	Ringo	Rockwell
Rhett	Rinzen	Rocky
Rhisiart	Riordan	Rod
Rhodes	Ripley	Rodd
Rhodri	Rippringham	Roddie
Rhun	Rishab	Roddy
Rhydwyn	Rishi	Roden
Rhys	Rishley	Roderick
Rian	Rishon	Roderigo
Ric	Risley	Rodman
Richard	Riston	Rodney
Rich	Ritchell	Rodolf
Richeman	Ritchie	Rodolfo
Richman	Ritter	Rodrigo
Rick	Rivers	Rodrigue
Ricker	Rizal	Rodwell
Rickhill	Roald	Rogan
Rickworth	Roan	Rogelio

Roger	Ross	Rufford
Rohan	Roswald	Rufus
Rohit	Roth	Rugby
Rokus	Rothwell	Ruggenall
Roland	Rourke	Ruggwain
Roldan	Rous	Ruhinda
Rolf	Routledge	Rumford
Rolleston	Rowdon	Runako
Rollo	Rowe	Rune
Roly	Rowell	Rupert
Roman	Rowland	Rupesh
Romeo	Rowlett	Rurik
Romney	Rowley	Rusch
Romulus	Rowse	Rush
Ronak	Rowson	Rushford
Ronald	Roxbury	Ruskin
Ronan	Roy	Russ
Rondel	Royce	Russel
Rongo	Roydon	Russell
Roni	Royston	Rusty
Ronin	Ruark	Rutger
Ronit	Ruben	Rutherford
Ronson	Rubens	Rutland
Ront	Rubin	Rutledge
Rooney	Ruchir	Rutley
Roosevelt	Rudd	Ry
Roper	Rudhall	Ryall
Rory	Rudi	Ryan
Roscoe	Rudolph	Rycroft
Rosencrantz	Rudy	Ryder
Roshan	Rudyard	Rylan
Roslin	Ruel	Ryle

Ryley
Rylie
Ryman
Ryoichi
Ryozo
Ryton
Ryuichi

"S"

Saben
Sabir
Sabola
Sabre
Sacha
Sachchit
Sacheverell
Sachiel
Sachin
Sackville
Sadi
Sadik
Sadler
Sadurni
Safak
Safford
Sagar
Sage
Sagiv
Sahadev
Sahale

Sahara
Sahen
Sahib
Sahnan
Saidi
Saintaubin
Saintjohn
Sakda
Sakima
Salah
Salerio
Salford
Salim
Salisbury
Salman
Saloman
Salomo
Salomon
Salter
Salton
Saltonstall
Salvador
Salvatore
Sam
Samien
Samir
Sammie
Sammon
Sammy
Sampath
Sampson
Samson

Samudra
Samuel
Samuell
Sanat
Sanborn
Sanburne
Sancho
Sandeep
Sanders
Sandie
Sandler
Sandon
Sandor
Sandy
Sandys
Sanford
Sanjay
Sanjeev
Sanjog
Sankara
Sansom
Sansone
Santiago
Santo
Santon
Santos
Santosh
Santoso
Sapan
Sarasvan
Sarat
Sargent

Sarkis	Schuyler	Seleucus
Sarngin	Scipio	Selig
Sarni	Scobahull	Selim
Sarojin	Scolfield	Selwyn
Sarosh	Scott	Semih
Sasha	Scroggs	Sempronius
Saswata	Scrope	Semyon
Satayu	Scully	Senach
Satruijt	Seabert	Senajit
Saturnino	Seaborne	Senan
Saturninus	Seabrook	Sencer
Satyen	Sealey	Senichi
Saudeep	Seamus	Sennett
Saul	Sean	Senon
Saunak	Seanan	Septimus
Saunders	Searle	Serafino
Saunderson	Seaton	Seraphim
Saunterton	Sebastian	Serche
Saurabh	Sebes	Serge
Saviero	Secundus	Sergeant
Savill	Sedgewick	Sergent
Saville	Sedgley	Sergio
Sawyer	Sedley	Sergius
Sawyl	Seeley	Servan
Saxby	Seely	Sesto
Saxon	Seff	Seth
Saxton	Sefton	Setiawan
Sayed	Seger	Seton
Sayer	Seif	Seung
Saynsberry	Seiichi	Sevastian
Scarcliff	Selby	Sever
Scarus	Seldon	Severin

Severino	Shantanu	Shigekazu
Severn	Sharad	Shiloh
Sevilin	Sharif	Shilton
Seville	Sharma	Shima
Seward	Sharman	Shimon
Sexton	Shashi	Shing
Sextus	Shashwat	Shingleton
Seyed	Shaughan	Shinichi
Seymour	Shaun	Shipley
Seys	Shaw	Shipton
Seyton	Shawe	Shipwash
Sezni	Shay	Shishir
Shadwell	Shea	Shiv
Shafiq	Sheehan	Shiva
Shah	Sheffield	Shiveley
Shahar	Shelby	Shlomo
Shailen	Sheldon	Shmuel
Shailesh	Shelley	Shoesmith
Shakar	Shen	Shoichi
Shakir	Shepherd	Sholto
Shalabh	Sher	Shomari
Shalin	Sheraton	Shorditch
Shallow	Sherborne	Shotbolt
Shalom	Sherbourne	Shrey
Shaman	Sheridan	Shuichi
Shamus	Sheridon	Shulamith
Shanahan	Sherlock	Shunichi
Shandy	Sherman	Shunnar
Shane	Shern	Shvetank
Shankar	Sherwin	Shyam
Shanley	Sherwood	Shylock
Shannon	Shevington	Siamak

Sibbell	Sinnett	Snug
Siddartha	Sinnott	Socrates
Siddel	Siva	Sofronio
Siddharth	Sivan	Soham
Sidell	Siward	Sol
Sidney	Skeet	Solan
Siegbert	Skelly	Solanio
Siegfried	Skelton	Solinus
Sigebryht	Skene	Solomon
Sigfried	Skern	Solon
Siggy	Skipp	Solt
Sigi	Skipper	Solyom
Sigmund	Skipwith	Soma
Sigurd	Skjold	Somerled
Silas	Sklaer	Somerset
Siler	Slade	Somerville
Silvanus	Slate	Sonam
Silvester	Sleaford	Sonnagh
Silvio	Slender	Sonny
Silvius	Slevin	Sophocles
Simeon	Sloan	Soren
Similien	Sly	Sorley
Simmons	Slyfield	Sorrell
Simon	Smedley	Soterios
Simonides	Smith	Sotton
Simple	Snayth	Southwell
Simpson	Snehal	Spalding
Sinan	Snell	Sparke
Sinbad	Snelling	Sparrow
Sinclair	Snorre	Spebbington
Singh	Snout	Speed
Sinjon	Snowden	Speir

Spelman	Stanley	Stig
Spence	Stan	Stiles
Spencer	Stanton	Stille
Spettell	Stanwick	Stillman
Spicer	Stanwix	Stinson
Spike	Staple	Stiofan
Spiridon	Starbuck	Stockley
Sprottle	Starr	Stockton
Sprunt	Starveling	Stoddard
Squire	Staunton	Stoddeley
Sridhar	Staverton	Stoke
Srijan	Stavros	Stokerton
Srikant	Stedman	Stokes
Srinath	Steele	Stokey
Srinivas	Stefan	Stokley
Sriram	Stefanos	Stone
Stack	Steffan	Stoner
Stacy	Stein	Storm
Staffan	Sten	Storr
Stafford	Stenton	Stoughton
Stamford	Stephan	Stowe
Stanbury	Stephano	Stoyan
Standen	Stephen	Strachleigh
Standish	Stepney	Strader
Standon	Sterling	Strahan
Stanfield	Sterne	Strangewayes
Stanford	Stert	Stratford
Stanhope	Steve	Strato
Stanislaus	Steven	Stratton
Stanislav	Stevenson	Street
Stanislaw	Steward	Strelley
Stanko	Stewart	Strom

Stroud
Stu
Stuart
Stubb
Studs
Sturt
Styles
Subodh
Sudarshan
Sudesha
Sudeva
Sudhansu
Sudhir
Sudi
Suffield
Sugriva
Sukarman
Sukumar
Sulaiman
Suleiman
Sulio
Sullivan
Sully
Sulwyn
Sulyard
Sumadhur
Suman
Sumantu
Sumati
Sumit
Sumner
Sun

Sundara
Sunil
Suresh
Surony
Surya
Sutcliffe
Sutherland
Sutton
Suvrata
Svein
Sven
Swagat
Swain
Swan
Swapnil
Sweeney
Sweeny
Sweetecok
Swetenham
Swindon
Swinford
Swithin
Switt
Sycamore
Sydenham
Sykes
Sylvain
Sylvan
Sylvester
Symon
Synclair
Syrus

Szabolcs
Szalok
Szemere
Szervoc
Szesco
Szevor
Szilord
Szolot
Szylve
Szymon

"T"

Taavi
Tab
Tabansi
Tabard
Tabari
Tabb
Tabor
Tad
Tadc
Tadd
Taddeo
Tadi
Taffy
Taggart
Tahir
Tai

Tailer	Tannar	Teague
Tailor	Tanner	Teal
Tait	Tano	Tean
Tajo	Tapan	Tearlach
Takai	Tapesh	Tecer
Takoda	Tara	Tecwyn
Taksa	Tarang	Ted
Taksony	Tarasios	Tedcastle
Taku	Tarcal	Teddie
Talbot	Tardos	Teddy
Talfryn	Taree	Tee
Talib	Tariq	Tej
Taliesin	Tarjan	Telford
Tallis	Tarkan	Telo
Talman	Tarn	Tem
Talon	Taro	Teman
Talorg	Tarquin	Temani
Talos	Tarrant	Templar
Tam	Tarun	Tenenan
Tama	Tas	Tennyson
Tamas	Tashi	Tenzin
Tame	Tate	Tenzing
Tamer	Tathal	Teodor
Tamir	Tathan	Tercan
Tancred	Tatum	Terence
Tancredo	Taurin	Terje
Tane	Taurinus	Terrel
Tanek	Taurus	Terrence
Taner	Tavis	Terrie
Tangaroa	Tavish	Terro
Tangwyn	Tawhiri	Terry
Tanicus	Taylor	Tetony

Teulyddog	Thorbjorn	Tibbord
Tewdwr	Thorburn	Tiberius
Tex	Thord	Tibold
Tezer	Thore	Tiernan
Thabit	Thorfinn	Tierney
Thaddeaus	Thorgeirr	Tihamar
Thaddeus	Thorgils	Tiki
Thai	Thorgrim	Tilak
Thaliard	Thorkell	Tilford
Thaman	Thorleifr	Tilghman
Than	Thormund	Tim
Thane	Thornburgh	Timeus
Thanos	Thorne	Timoleon
Thatcher	Thornley	Timon
Theobald	Thornton	Timor
Theobold	Thorpe	Timothy
Theodore	Thorstein	Timur
Theodoric	Thorulffr	Tindall
Theon	Thorvald	Tinh
Theophilus	Thorvid	Tipene
Theron	Thosa	Tiploft
Thersites	Thrandr	Titus
Theseus	Throckmorton	Titusz
Thibaud	Thurborn	Tivadar
Thidias	Thurio	Tivon
Thierry	Thurlow	Tobias
Thies	Thursby	Tobie
Thijs	Thurso	Toby
Thomas	Thurstan	Tod
Thor	Thurston	Todd
Thorald	Tibald	Toft
Thoralf	Tibalt	Toker

Tolga	Townsend	Tristram
Tom	Toyo	Troilus
Tomaj	Tracy	Trowbridge
Tomas	Trahaearn	Troy
Tomasz	Traherne	Truman
Tome	Tran	Trumpington
Tomi	Tranio	Tryggvi
Tomkin	Tranter	Trystan
Tommy	Travis	Tuart
Tomo	Trefor	Tuathal
Tong	Trefusis	Tubal
Tony	Tregonwell	Tubney
Topsfield	Trelawney	Tucker
Tor	Tremayne	Tudfwlch
Tore	Tremeur	Tudi
Torin	Trenowyth	Tudor
Tormey	Trent	Tudur
Tormod	Trenus	Tugdual
Torquil	Tresco	Tujan
Torr	Trethowan	Tuncer
Torrance	Trevelyan	Tungyr
Torrington	Trevett	Ture
Torsten	Trevor	Turi
Torvald	Trey	Turiau
Toste	Trigve	Turner
Tostig	Trilby	Turpin
Totthill	Trinculo	Tushar
Touchstone	Trinity	Tuvya
Toussaint	Tripp	Tuyen
Tovi	Trisanu	Twain
Town	Tristan	Twarby
Townley	Tristen	Tweedy

Twyford
Tyack
Tybalt
Tycho
Tye
Tyee
Tyler
Tymon
Tynan
Tyne
Tyrek
Tyrell
Tyrol
Tyrone
Tyrus
Tyson
Tytus
Tzuriel

"U"

Uba
Ubul
Udeh
Udell
Udit
Udo
Udolf
Uehudah
Ufford

Ufuk
Ugo
Ugod
Ugor
Ugur
Uilleam
Uisdean
Uland
Ulbrecht
Ulf
Ulffr
Ulfred
Ulmer
Ulprus
Ulrich
Ultan
Ulucan
Ulysses
Umar
Umberto
Unai
Underhill
Unni
Unton
Unwin
Upen
Upendra
Upor
Upravda
Upton
Upwood
Urban

Uren
Uri
Uriah
Urie
Uriel
Urien
Urjavaha
Uros
Ursel
Urson
Urswick
Urvan
Usamah
Ushnisha
Usko
Usman
Utah
Utt
Uttam
Uttanka
Utz
Uwain
Uwan
Uwe
Uxio
Uyeda
Uzi
Uzor
Uzziah

"V"

Vitoz
Vittore
Vittorio
Vitus
Vivatma
Vivek
Vivian
Vladilen
Vladimir
Vladislav
Volf
Volker
Volney
Voltimand
Vortigern
Voteporix
Vougay
Vyasa
Vyvyan

"W"

Wade
Wadham
Wagner
Wahib
Wahnond

Wain
Waine
Wainwright
Waite
Wake
Wakefield
Wakeman
Walby
Walchelim
Waldegrave
Waldeley
Waldemar
Walden
Waldo
Walenty
Waleran
Walford
Walid
Walker
Wallace
Walmer
Walpole
Walrond
Walsch
Walsh
Walter
Waltham
Walton
Walwyn
Waman
Wang
Wantell

Warbulton
Warburton
Ward
Warde
Wardell
Wardyworth
Warfield
Warley
Warmund
Warner
Warra
Warrain
Warren
Warrigal
Warrun
Warton
Warwick
Waseem
Washington
Wasim
Wassily
Watkin
Watson
Waverley
Waverly
Wayde
Wayland
Wayne
Wayte
Webb
Webster
Weeks

Welbeck	Wheeler	Willcotts
Welby	Whetu	William
Welch	Whit	Williams
Welcome	Whitby	Willie
Weldon	Whitcombe	Willis
Welford	White	Willmer
Wellington	Whitewood	Willoughby
Wellins	Whitfield	Wilmer
Wells	Whitford	Wilmot
Welsh	Whitley	Wilson
Wen	Whitmore	Wilton
Wenceslas	Whitney	Wim
Wendell	Whittaker	Winchester
Wendron	Whitton	Windham
Wenlock	Whowood	Windsor
Wenman	Whyting	Wingfield
Wensley	Wickham	Winkle
Wentworth	Wid	Winog
Werner	Widdowson	Winslow
Wesley	Wieslav	Winston
West	Wightman	Winstringham
Westbrook	Wihtred	Winter
Westlake	Wilbur	Winthrop
Weston	Wiley	Winton
Westwood	Wilford	Wirrin
Wetherby	Wilfred	Wiseman
Wetherden	Wilkes	Wistan
Wexcombe	Wilkie	Withinghall
Weylin	Wilkins	Witton
Weymouth	Will	Wolf
Wheatley	Willard	Wolfden
Wheaton	Willardsey	Wolfe

Wolfgang
Wolfram
Wolstonton
Wolter
Wolton
Wood
Woodbrygg
Woodburn
Woodley
Woodrow
Woodward
Woody
Woorak
Woorin
Worcester
Worsley
Wotton
Wreke
Wren
Wrenn
Wright
Wulfhere
Wulfnoth
Wyard
Wyatt
Wyber
Wyburn
Wye
Wyghtham
Wykeham
Wylde
Wylie

Wyman
Wymer
Wyndam
Wyndham
Wynford
Wynn
Wynston
Wynton
Wyome
Wyville

"X"

Xan
Xanthus
Xanti
Xavier
Xenophon
Xenos
Xerxes
Xiao
Ximen
Ximenes
Ximens
Ximun
Xurxo
Xylon

"Y"

Yate
Yaxley
Yelverton
Yornold
Young

"Z"

Zabulon
Zaccheo
Zachariah
Zacharias
Zachary
Zadok
Zador
Zafar
Zafer
Zagger
Zagon
Zahin
Zahir
Zahneny
Zahur
Zaid
Zaide
Zajzon
Zakai
Zaki

Zale	Zeko	Zobor
Zalen	Zelig	Zoello
Zalman	Zelipe	Zoilo
Zamir	Zelman	Zoland
Zamor	Zelotes	Zoltan
Zander	Zenas	Zombor
Zane	Zennor	Zoran
Zanebono	Zeno	Zoroaster
Zani	Zenoa	Zorro
Zaniel	Zenobio	Zosimo
Zanipolo	Zenon	Zotico
Zann	Zenos	Zowie
Zanobi	Zephan	Zsigmond
Zared	Zephaniah	Zsolt
Zarek	Zeren	Zubin
Zarend	Zerind	Zuriel
Zavier	Zero	Zurl
Zayden	Zeroun	
Zazu	Zetany	
Zbigniew	Zeth	
Zdenek	Zeus	
Zebadiah	Zev	
Zebedeo	Zia	
Zebulon	Ziff	
Zebulun	Ziggy	
Zechariah	Zigmond	
Zedekiah	Zigmund	
Zedock	Zion	
Zeeman	Zircon	
Zefirino	Ziv	
Zeke	Ziven	
Zeki	Zoard	

Coming Soon!!!

Name Your Heroine

and

Name Your Villain

www.ingramcontent.com/pod-product-compliance
Lightning Source LLC
Chambersburg PA
CBHW060147050426
42448CB00010B/2345